THE ART & VOICE OF AUTISM

Written by
GINA URICCHIO

Illustrated by
ALLY URICCHIO

Uricchio, Gina, and Uricchio, Ally, *Mother Asana: The Art and Voice of Autism*

All rights reserved.
Copyright © 2022 by Gina Uricchio
Art by Ally Uricchio
Layout and design by Crystal Cregge, Liona Design Co. http://lionadesignco.com/
Published by KWE Publishing www.kwepub.com

No part of this book may be reproduced in any form or by any electronic or mechanical means, including information storage and retrieval systems, without written permission from the author or publisher, except for the use of brief quotations in a book review.

ISBNs: Paperback 978-1-950306-82-4, Ebook 978-1-950306-83-1
Library of Congress Catalog Number: 2021923449

To support local communities, raise awareness and provide funds, Mother Asana donates proceeds from books sales to autism awareness organizations. Get involved today! Visit motherasana.com/about

Join the Mother Asana community! Visit us at www.motherasana.com for updates, blogs, amazing products, and more. We'd love to hear from you. Shine on!

KWE Publishing LLC.
www.kwepub.com

To my family, John, Ally, and Johnny, and to every family that lives in a house that houses autism.

> I love you, not for what you are, but what I am when I am with you.
> —ELIZABETH BARRETT BROWNING

To my parents, Peter and Julia, for allowing art and creative inspiration into a young girl's life and letting me be free.

MOTHER ASANA

TABLE OF CONTENTS

SUMMER

Shine artwork 9
"Mr. Sun" 10
Shine! Journal Prompt 11
Summer Movies & Menus 12
We're All Spinning On The Same Ball artwork 13
"We're All Spinning On The Same Ball" 14
Create the Earth 15
Beach Picnic Menu 16
Summer School artwork 17
"Summer School" 18
Summer School Journal Prompts 19
The Beach Rocks artistic expression 20

FALL

The Sad Is Over artwork 21
"The Sad Is Over" 22
The Sad Is Over Journal Prompt 23
Art Museum Visit And Recreate Your Favorite Artist's Masterpiece 24
Party Hats On artwork 25
"Party Hats On" 26
Party Hats On Journal Prompts 27
Holiday Gift List 28
Family Tree artwork 29
"Family Tree" 30
New Year, New Word Journal Prompt 31
Cookie Basket Creations artistic expression 32

WINTER

Snowball artwork 33

"Snowball" 34

Self-Care Journal Prompt 35

Winter Essential Oils For Grounding and Yoga Poses 36

Counting Miracles artwork 37

"Counting Miracles" 38

Counting Miracles Journal Prompt 39

Be Happy Valentine Chocolate Board artistic expression 40

SPRING

Bloom! artwork 41

"Choices Count" 42

Manifest Your Miracle Journal Prompt 43

Dream Spray 44

May All Beings Be Free! artwork 45

"Cereal Girl" 46

Watercolor Expression Journal Prompt 47

Cereal Rainbows artistic expression 48

References 49, 50

HOW TO USE THIS BOOK

Namaste! And welcome. As you can tell, *Mother Asana: The Art and Voice of Autism* is not a traditional book. Just as families with autistic children have unique ways of experiencing their world, this book offers a unique way of approaching family time, super fun shared activities, real talk about real topics, and places to journal, doodle, and save your artwork and other keepsakes.

Our mission? To bring your family together at the kitchen table.
Or your living room. Or the room where you live.

Allow me to introduce us to you.

"I am her voice...she is my heart"

We are the mother-daughter team of Gina and Ally Uricchio. Through this book, we invite you to join our artistically designed universe challenged by autism life on the spectrum.

Our mission is to encourage and create awareness of the creative communication based on a mother-daughter bond and showcase a celebrated life.

This book is an extension of our world and lifestyle that we call "Mother Asana."

What is Mother Asana? And how do you use this book?

ART:

Together, we bring the focus of Ally's art and expression. Throughout these pages, enjoy Ally's original artwork and her fantastic view of the world.

YOGA AND INSIGHTS:

Enjoy Yogi Gina's yoga practice and meditation insights on how these practices have been the instrumental way in parenting and navigating life inside the autism spectrum.

ACTIVITIES:

Our entire family, including my husband John and son Johnny, along with Ally and me, enjoy relaxed, chill activities. Cook with us, celebrate with us, join us as we Inspire, Connect and Tune IN with each other, and families hurdling a life after an autism diagnosis.

THE ART & VOICE OF AUTISM

ALL OF THESE ELEMENTS ARE MOTHER ASANA.

Lovers of nature, we have organized the book by seasons. Summer, fall, spring, and winter contain special moments that we can savor and treasure.

Why does this book look different?

WE INTENTIONALLY CHOSE A BOOK THAT YOU CAN MAKE YOUR WAY. WHAT WE OFFER IS:

- A soft cover that feels good
- A book that can take some wear and tear
- A book that lays flat to make it easier to use
- A folder to capture your artwork, keepsakes
- A book that does not smudge when you write on it

HOW DO YOU MAKE IT YOUR OWN? HERE ARE A FEW SUGGESTIONS:

- After you create artwork, save it in the folder
- Write in the journals
- Experience the activities together
- Add your own artwork to the pages
- Express yourself however you like in the journal pages
- Keep this book where your family gathers—maybe it is the kitchen table

There are endless ways to use this book! Please share your ideas with us.

—GINA & ALLY

ABOUT THE AUTHOR

Gina Uricchio is a mother, visionary, and yogi. Creating connection is the cornerstone to her parenting & personal style. Meditation & yoga have been instrumental while raising a family alongside her husband John—especially meeting the challenges of a special needs child. Gina installs stillness, resilience & surrender everyday as a "warrior mom". She lives with her family in Connecticut and enjoys the many seasons of New England, especially summer. When not at home, you can find her at the beach, savoring a cup of coffee or exploring a local farmer's market.

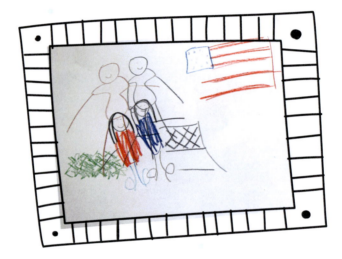

ABOUT THE ILLUSTRATOR

Ally Uricchio is an artist, a yogi, and a natural free spirit. A lover of music, water, and being playful, she spends her days living in each season with presence. Ally practices yoga daily by creating her own space with comfort—establishing safe energy for herself. Ally loves going to the beach and she's a non-stop giggler. When she is not drawing or singing, she enjoys going for long car rides, drive thrus, and any wide open space.

SUMMER

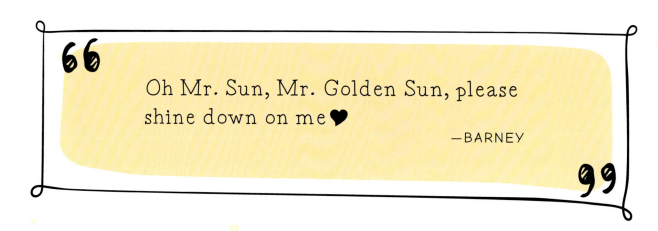

> Oh Mr. Sun, Mr. Golden Sun, please shine down on me ♥
>
> —BARNEY

 ## MR. SUN

June 21.

Summer Solstice.

Longest Day of Light.

On this calendar date we look back at the past few months—even far as the deep Winter—

And with reflection on what seeds we may have planted in our gardens and in our lives, the warmer months allow them to break open.

We've gone quiet, made soups, snuggled through snow storms and made snowmen. We've walked in the rain, planted pansies, and made tea.

And slowly now we turn our eyes to June 21—our longest day of light. We get surrounded by it. And here we let go once again. We watch what we planted burst open in our gardens and our worlds.

Through water, we see the efforts we used for our gardens.

Through our children, we see the efforts we've used this school year for parenting.

Through the finish of another school year, we see our children's growth.

Through loving more, trying harder, doing better, we see the efforts we've planted in our personal quiet space of our own life open.

We honor all of this.

As we go through these unscheduled lazier days let's trust the seeds we've planted.

Watch the blossoming.

Let it flow.

Sit back.

Wander.

Salute the sun.

Shine.

SUMMER

SHINE! JOURNAL PROMPT

We take summer very seriously around here. We have created a journal page here to inspire yourself and your family to engage in your summer heart.

1. What's your summer "bucket list"? What will you do before summer ends?

2. What is your ideal way to spend a summer day? List your favorite ways to spend a lazy summer afternoon.

ARTISTIC EXPRESSION
SUMMER MOVIES & MENUS

Here are some of our favorite family movies!

- E.T.
- Jaws
- Ferris Bueller's Day Off
- Grease
- Finding Dory
- The Little Mermaid

Here are some fuss-free menus! Everybody in the kitchen helps!

MAKE IT MEXICAN NIGHT: TACO AND FAJITA BAR

- Kids can help sort toppings
- Guacamole
- Salsa
- Tortilla chips
- Beans
- Selected proteins
- Rice

MINI DIRT CAKES

- Grab mini pails and shovels from your favorite dollar store
- Box of Oreos or chocolate wafer cookies
- Favorite whipped topping
- Flavored puddings of your choice
- Gummy worms
- Involve the kids to smash the cookies with a hammer in Ziploc bags and build their own cake

STRAWBERRY SHORTCAKE

- Biscuits: store bought or make your own
- Blueberries/strawberries or any summer fruit
- Strawberry ice cream

SUMMER

WE'RE ALL SPINNING ON THE SAME BALL

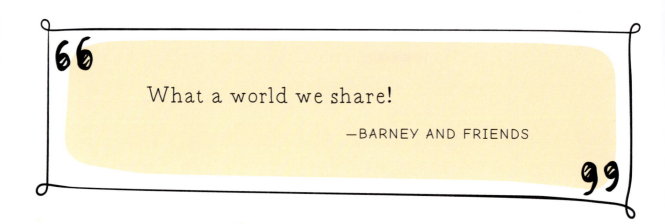

> What a world we share!
>
> —BARNEY AND FRIENDS

WE'RE ALL SPINNING ON THE SAME BALL

We are all alike. To notice that we are all the same is a very hard concept. Meditation teacher Pema Chodron talks about seeing ourselves in others—and learning how to pause and catch ourselves before we begin any sort of judgment. This, my friends, is never easy. I mean really...how can all these people around us essentially be "US"?

Within the world that my family navigates we have been subjected to judgment in the strangest places. The grocery store, the airport, and restaurants. Funny how people can stare you down and think you don't see them. Whether there was judgment facing us or not, I can assure you it never feels good. Most of the time it might be because Ally is singing Christmas carols in Walmart in July, or perhaps being stared at for crying in line at the grocery store while someone else gets to stand with a look of disapproval....As if we may actually listen to what they have to say. In these circumstances, I have felt judgement and wanted to literally lunge into some folks. I can stop myself and say that "we are all alike." We are all learning, figuring out new stuff all the time. We all need love, we all feel fear, we all have emotions.

We have all been on each side. Whether it's being judged or judging...Ally shows us to hold no prejudice. She knows nothing of why it would be wrong to sing about Christmas in July. Her way is through love, and when she encounters the judges or skeptics she literally laughs them off. This hasn't been easy for the rest of the family. Grocery stores and airports are all teaching environments and we have had our share of rude comments. But thankfully, with every person that falters, there always is a kind person right behind them.

This is what soothes us...lifts and elevates us, keeps our confidence rolling so we can continue the teaching.

And always the reminder. We are all alike. And according to Ally's favorite song..."We're all spinning on the same ball." We move from a place of comparison to a place of equanimity.

Let's try and practice that.

SUMMER

CREATE THE EARTH

This is a simple project using blue and green construction paper and glue.

- Draw a large circle to depict your earth.
- Now here's the fun part! Rip and tear up various squares of blue and green to fill the circle.
- Glue colored pieces inside the circle.

Share your artwork with us at @mother_asana.

SUMMER

ARTISTIC EXPRESSION

BEACH PICNIC MENU

- Favorite beach blanket
- Grab a portable cheese board that can travel!
- Assorted cheeses
- Crackers, mini cheese sandwich crackers, pretzels, summer fruits
- Chips of course! Truffle chips are my fave! (Trader Joe's truffle chips! And other yummy stuff!)

BEACH MUST HAVES

- Large beach totes for sunscreen and beach accessories: https://tinyurl.com/llbeantoteforfun
- Shovels and pails for castles and collecting shells
- Stocked cooler
- Tunes
- Sunglasses
- Giant beach hat
- Bucket hats or visor
- Money for the snack bar!!! It's all about the snacks!!

SUMMER

SUMMER
SCHOOL

SUMMER

> *Summer afternoon: To me those have always been the two most beautiful words in the English language.*
> —HENRY JAMES

SUMMER SCHOOL

My life right now isn't about a lot of applause. In fact, it is getting quieter...steadier.

Routine. Structure. In a house that houses autism we rely on a formula of schedules. We can watch things blow literally out of control without one, even if it's loosely based. Those are days where I may drop the ball on "the work." Autism is a puzzle piece that dangles daily in front of my third eye. It's a place where I have to rely on my intuition so much as a parent.

What to do next. How to respond...react. Sit back...or just sit and wait. Some days we are so locked down in the puzzle we can't find the connecting piece. And then out of nowhere, we are sitting, we quickly see it. There it is...the piece we are looking for connects us...finishes the section of many of the puzzles we are solving. It's the opening, the wide blue sky, the calm after the storm.

I write this on July 4th. That is where freedom lives. Freedom for our family. Freedom in the exhale. Freedom to sit and wait for the next thing. Sometimes it's days and others it is five minutes after we just linked our missing piece.

THE WORK. IT IS HARD. We don't break off in the summer. We often hear about doing the work as we grow older, rediscovering ourselves and connecting deeply with our soul's path & journey in this lifetime. We are getting schooled in a discipline for which we had no intention.

She looks at me this morning and says... "My life is YOUR life's work." ♥

THERE IT IS.

We often seek outside our own lives to attain jubilation. To look at other situations and think we may be happier there. For me, the puzzle piece quickly comes back to focus. It's hard to separate ourselves from OUR WORK. But THIS SPACE is when we find the gold treasure we are sitting on. This life with Autism, it resembles nothing my husband and I had planned for our future, for ourselves as a young couple. My son was born into it. As a family, we are constantly a movement of expansion, of learning, and becoming.

THIS IS OUR WORK. EVERYDAY IS OUR CLASSROOM.

SUMMER 00

SUMMER SCHOOL JOURNAL PROMPTS

1. Who are you trying to connect with?

2. What puzzles are you currently solving or need to solve?

SUMMER

ARTISTIC EXPRESSION

THE BEACH ROCKS

I love this project on a misty summer morning when everyone is looking for structure. It will satisfy even the most distracted family members.

WHAT TO DO FOR THIS PROJECT:

Collect rocks of all kinds, shapes and sizes. Smooth beach rocks are our first choice.

Don't have rocks? Not near a beach? No worries! These days you can even buy rocks at home improvement stores or on your favorite online shopping sites.

SHOPPING LIST:

- Paint brushes
- Non-toxic paints/glitter
- Mod-Podge for sealing

After you complete your artwork, add Mod-Podge. Allow to dry.

WHAT WE LOVE TO PAINT:

The sky is the limit! Summertime ideas include:

- Watermelon design
- Anchors
- Flags
- Ice cream cones
- Rainbows
- Moon and stars
- Emoji faces

HOW TO ENJOY AND DISPLAY:

- Use as place setting
- Enjoy as paper weights all year
- Add to your garden or outside
- As a creative design at your kitchen table

 # THE SAD IS OVER

Breathe.   I can't Breathe.

Stop holding your Breath.   Meditate.

Practice Yoga.   Drink Tea.

Walk in Circles.   Repeat 2x daily.

Write…Write…wait a minute. My friends say you should really put this into words. No, really people, I have circles to walk.

More Tea.   More Breathing.

I had cancer.   Breast Cancer.

Diagnosed January 25, 2013, on most freezing cold January day and let me tell you: Cancer is fast. Routine ultrasound on Monday. Biopsy on Wednesday. Cancer diagnosis and sitting in the surgeon's office Friday afternoon. Cancer waits for nothing or no one. It doesn't care if you have a trip to go on—a birthday, a party—or if you just have your everyday rounds to get done.

Nope.

Cancer just barges in and TRIES to take you and swallow your family up with it.

I was saved by my ultrasound. Divine Intervention —truly—every rosary said by my grandmothers plus every medal and holy water they bestowed upon me. I had early stage breast cancer. To be technical, "invasive lobular breast cancer Stage one." 2 small tumors. Doctor says you could never feel them.

My husband John is the most gracious, patient, and generous man. He and I meet with the doctor, we get the details, we get to make the decisions, and we walk to the car to drive home. It is freezing cold and I feel nothing.

We can learn every thing there is to know, where to get healed and tell our kids and our parents and friends AND get everybody to school on time.

We opt for bilateral mastectomy with reconstruction. One large surgery with 6-8 week recovery time, then two smaller surgeries to finish reconstruction. One in August. Another in November.

It is January 28…The phone rings for six weeks straight. Relatives. And I have a lot of them…Brazil is calling, Italy is calling, Friends are calling, and Doctors are calling. More test results from your tumor. Checking to see if I am estrogen receptive, checking to see if I am Her2 positive, BRCA gene testing, bloodwork, preop, "let's go over the surgery again" talks, meet the plastic surgeon.

Need some tea yet?

Which leads me to my coffee. I have cancer… I should probably assess my way of eating. Hmmm. I'm pretty much considered the healthy one around my friends and family. Ugh…I can't give coffee the old heave ho! But I guess I can let Tea move in…Chai and Green tea become some choices…Cue the Kale, Collards and Chards and every colored veg in the rainbow into my trusty Vitamix…Add the anti-inflammatory…but the most important thing is learning to TRUST my body…and learn I can live, love and feel full with all types of food. Yup that means All Food.

AND…Everyday I had to make sure I was breathing. Conscious breathing, In fact, let's all take a big breath right now.

I get my surgeries. I do my stuff. And what does that little light girl Ally do when this is all going on? She starts singing and playing the Christian hymn "Shine Jesus Shine" every day.

And when we get our biopsies and diagnoses all tied up—she looks at me and says, "THE SAD IS OVER."

And that's what she says—and I look at her and say…"It is over, Al. Mommy's here. Mommy is good…All good. Let's go get some fries 🍟!!!"

FALL 00

> "You're going to make it. Trust me." —PSALM 23

THE SAD IS OVER JOURNAL PROMPT

We've all encountered difficult situations within ourselves or our families. One strategy I've had is always relying on my personal strength, faith, and Ally's freedom to begin over and over.

- In what ways has sadness entered your life? Where does it reside?
- Where do you let it go when it takes up too much room?
- Who inspires you?

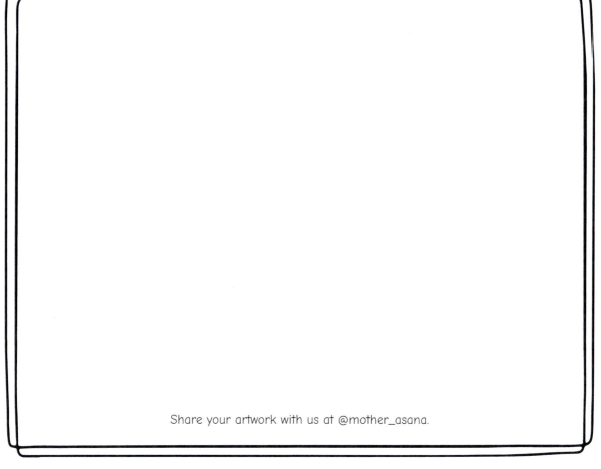

Share your artwork with us at @mother_asana.

FALL

ARTISTIC EXPRESSION

ART MUSEUM VISIT AND RECREATE YOUR FAVORITE ARTIST'S MASTERPIECE

Here are some art museums—visit them online or in person—and recreate your own favorite artist's masterpiece like Ally did below of Monet's waterlilies.

On a chilly fall day, why not go on a virtual visit? All of the museums are available to visit online!

ART MUSEUM VISIT

- Dr. Seuss, Springfield, MA
  http://www.seussinspringfield.org/
- Eric Carle Museum, Amherst, MA
  https://www.carlemuseum.org/
- Discovery Place, Charlotte, NC
  https://www.discoveryplace.org/
- Boston Children's Museum, Boston, MA
  https://bostonchildrensmuseum.org/
- Imagine Van Gogh, Boston MA and Tacoma/Seattle, WA
  https://www.imagine-vangogh.com
- Detroit Institute of Art, Detroit, MI
  https://www.dia.org/
- Children's Museum of Manhattan, New York, NY
  https://cmom.org/
- Charles Schulz Museum, Santa Rosa, CA
  https://schulzmuseum.org/
- Children's Museums in East Coast from Trip Savvy
  https://www.tripsavvy.com/childrens-museums-virtual-visit-4800065

FALL

PARTY HATS ON

FALL

> "It's impossible," said Pride.
> "It's risky," said Experience.
> "It's pointless," said Reason.
> "Give it a try," whispered the Heart.
>
> —UNKNOWN

Fall brings in both my kids' birthdays. They are close together in years and months. I found myself with a party hat on for three months! In our home, not only are there the big celebratory days, but we celebrate the simple moments with the expression "Party Hats On!" such as a graduation from preschool, a new job offer, a simple plane ride with no screaming, when your child gets their driver's license, to a successful trip to the dentist. "Party Hats On" lives in all these situations.

 ## PARTY HATS ON

Together today we are on a walk.

Literally.

We walk into the next situation.

"Here's what we'll do" I say....

A verbal cue... I hear myself speak and the schedule rolls out quickly.

"We will walk to the beach."

"We can touch the water."

"We can look for seashells and then we can get an ice cream."

"Then we will go back home and be 'all done.'"

Together we walk.

We have gotten side-swiped a few times.

Stuck. Sitting on the side of the road.

On the sidelines of our journey, not knowing what's next.

A mother who is part teacher, and a daughter who is a master.

"Don't WORRY," she says. She knows exactly where she wants to go. AND I have my hidden agenda for her. I want her to try this, go here, stay longer...

I move too fast sometimes, so I am told.

For this mother and daughter team I have to slow it way down. We have a lifetime of adult learning together.

Together we walk.

"Take a LEFT," she says.

Let me leave the work of trying so hard, I pray to myself. Instead let me be present with my sweet girl.

No add ons, no sneaky corners.

The art of simplicity.

Let us let life unfold as our feet hit the sand.

TOMORROW SHE WALKS.... by herself in her cap and gown with twenty years of special educational programming behind her.

She will walk by herself. She's proud. She knows we are going to do some good stuff together.

Party Hats ON Al!

Our journey of A D U L T I N G is just beginning!

FALL 00

PARTY HATS ON JOURNAL PROMPTS

1. What everyday victories are you celebrating?

2. Here is a place to record how you celebrate your Party Hats On moments!

FALL

ARTISTIC EXPRESSION

HOLIDAY GIFT LIST

We've compiled a list because at this time of year, we have so much gratitude for our:

- caregivers
- babysitters
- teachers
- paraprofessionals
- family
- and besties in our lives!

HERE ARE SOME SWEET GIFT IDEAS FOR THE SWEET PEOPLE IN OUR LIVES!

- Lunch coolers
- Beach tote
- Painted rocks with pretty napkins
- Popcorn popper with suggested movie list
- Wind chimes
- Hanging basket of flowers

FAMILY TREE

> 🎵 A family is people, A family is love, that's a family,
> ...... Yeah mine's just right for me...
> ...... Yeah mine's just right for me! ♥🎵
>
> —BARNEY

FAMILY TREE

As families, how do we learn and grow? We continue to mature and trust year after year in the company of each other. Four people. Four different directions. Each member touches down daily in a separate world "doing their thing" and then somehow at the end of the day we find ourselves around the family kitchen table to regroup.

As families we go through stuff together and sometimes we need to work it out on our own. Children mature. Parents step back.

We give each other space.

And then just like that—we are all back at the table. We regroup. We confide. We fit each other. We share our victories, our fears...there are sounds of laughter...Ally's happy sounds, as we like to call them.

In our house even on the darkest day, the table gets set. Salad is made. Pasta boils and comforts. We fill up. We fill our bodies and our hearts with unconditional love.

Sometimes the chatter, sometimes the silence, tech interruptions and so forth. The table, this family accepts all of it.

The family table provides the stability we need to walk away each day.

To begin,

To finish something,

To say goodbye,

And most of all, to welcome and open our hearts.

YES.

♪ A family is people, a family is love, and mine's just right for me! ♪

NEW YEAR, NEW WORD JOURNAL PROMPT

As you look back on your year, take space for yourself here to record your favorite moments. What you achieved, conquered, and any unexpected places you never thought you would travel to.

Choose a word for yourself for the new year to come. Spend some time revisiting the dreams you manifested. Take inventory of the way the beauty in life unfolded for you.

Take some time and visit this page each year.

Share your artwork with us at @mother_asana.

ARTISTIC EXPRESSION

COOKIE BASKET CREATIONS—BAKE, DECORATE, OR BUY COOKIES FOR A COOKIE PARTY

Find cute containers for the cookies to take away. Find a few and decorate with stickers or glitter pens.

SOME OF OUR FAVORITES:

- Mexican Tea Cakes
- Candy Cane Cookies — food coloring, sugar and cookie dough
- Sugar Cookies
- Italian Chocolate Cookies
- Peanut Butter Kiss Cookies
- Seven Layer Bars
- Italian White Cookies
- These are all available as recipes online or transform store bought cookies as well with sprinkles, frosting, crushed peppermint, and whatever your sweet tooth desires!
- For more family recipes and cookie ideas, go to: www.motherasana.com

WINTER

> **"** I knew who I was this morning but I've changed a few times since then...
>
> —ALICE IN WONDERLAND **"**

 ## SNOWBALL

Winter, dear old friend. I have known you for so long. We have shared so many storms and unseasonable days where we have not been ourselves.

One thing is true. You show up no matter what & give me permission to rest.

For our family to meet up with that weighted winter feeling means we must gather our fall harvest & finally leave our beloved summer behind. We drift to nesting.

Our bodies begin to insulate, we add layers, we begin to romanticize about wearing layers—our favorite cardigans and flannels.

And our children...whatever their age they keep us going.

No matter how high the snow there must be a schedule of some sort. And on a good old-fashioned New England snow day, once we are plowed out we hit it.

The Drive Thru.

It's easy.

It's warm.

Plus it wins accolades with Ally.

Transitions one part of the day to the next...Funny thing is, it helps me too.

We regroup.

We roll the windows down.

Turn the heat on high and catch a few flakes.

We take in our WINTER.

We are reset. We acknowledge the energy shift—how we change our minds & preferences moment to moment.

When we pull back home, we are back to balance. Fresh faced from the cool air & wind.

We feel lighter & free.

We inject the FLOW in our day.

We can decide our vibe.

Our intention and attention to energy flow is essential to keep up & keep us going.

WINTER

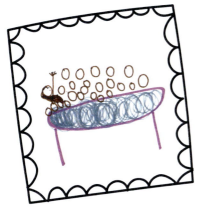

SELF-CARE JOURNAL PROMPT

Self-compassion is taking care of yourself. And we all need our get-away time.

How do you keep your summer heart alive in winter?

WINTER

ARTISTIC EXPRESSION

WINTER ESSENTIAL OILS FOR GROUNDING

Essential oils are a marvelous way to transition yourself from one mood to another. We use them in diffusers, as aromatherapy and often on the bottoms of our feet. Some of our favorites are:

ORANGE
- For uplift and bringing the sunshine in on a winter day. It's a reviving and fresh mood lifter.

VETIVER
- Often called the sedative oil, this one is great for clearing tension, calming your nervous system, and relieving stress and anxiety.
- Swipe some on the bottoms of your feet or the back of your neck. Applying oils on the feet can help to keep us calm and less anxious which can promote a better night's sleep.

GERANIUM
- Used for anxiety and depression, this floral oil offers comfort during stressful times. We love to use it in a diffuser.

FRANKINCENSE
- Like Saran wrap for the body, this oil offers full protection. Help quiet yourself and your mind with this oil.

ALLY'S YOGA POSES:

GROUNDING YOGA FLOW SUKHASANA

SUNBREATHS

MOUNTAIN

WARRIOR 1

WARRIOR 2

SEATFORWARD FOLD

CHILD

SHIVISANA

WINTER

COUNTING MIRACLES

WINTER

> **"** I carry your heart...I carry it in my heart
>
> —E.E. CUMMINGS **"**

COUNTING MIRACLES

My prayer from A Course in Miracles is—

WHERE would you have me go?

WHAT would you have me do?

WHAT would you have me say and to WHOM?

And each day I know I can choose to be reset for the miraculous or hide under the shroud of my ego. The COURSE says that's where hell resides.

We all do it, slip into the low vibe. Could be a visit to the pantry for chocolate or a Netflix binge, a drive thru for a salted caramel latte with extra caramel or an old story of frustration, placed on rotation in my head.

Sometimes it's because of our company we keep...Many times it is the news these days. And a LOT of times it's our choice.

Worrying, constrictions, hard ways: turns out these ways are not my ways.

I know I can make choices. My practice teaches me. We begin again. With each inhale there is another shot. In the midst of parenting, and learning adulting with Ally, I witness how often I get stuck. Trying too hard, trying to make it right for her. It comes down to control. Let me look for a miracle in this tiny moment. But the miracle can't come if I block it with my ego.

I need to free up space. I need to bust through the block so I can get to the other side.

I leave the low vibe behind. I close the pantry and go to my front steps. I get in touch with Mother Nature. Big breath in and AGAIN. I tune into my body to open my practice. I salute all the teachers who have come before me, asking my angels and guides to enter into this space. I choose breath of fire. I inhale and then exhale quickly through my nose, finishing with a DEEP inhale, and finally exhaling for 1-3 minutes.

Hands come together as I bow to myself and all that is so much bigger than me. I am refreshed. My energy is aligned.

TODAY she runs off the bus, so happy—and in a loud voice shouts "Counting Miracles!" with a piece of paper held tightly in her hand.

That's it. No other words.

I take the paper and look down. "Counting Miracles" it says in her handwriting.

YES. That's what we need to do; we can count miracles. Because they come all day long. In fact they overlap each other.

There really is No time for the EGO in between miracles. ☺

COUNTING MIRACLES
JOURNAL PROMPT

"Manifest Your Miracle"

What are you keeping? What are you leaving behind? What words define your winter?

WINTER

ARTISTIC EXPRESSION

BE HAPPY VALENTINE CHOCOLATE BOARD

This is an easy, satisfying treat to create with your family. Everyone can help! Candy shopping is always fun. Assembly inspires creativity and the results? Smiles all around!

TO PREPARE:

- Bring out your favorite serving platter! Ours is a heart-shaped wooden board.
- Shop for your favorite treats. We've listed our favorites, but be sure to customize for your family's dietary needs and preferences.
  - Chocolate cookies
  - Caramels
  - Chocolate covered pretzels
  - Hand dipped rice krispie treats
  - Chocolate covered blueberries or raisins
  - Chocolate covered gummy bears
  - Chocolate hearts
  - Dried fruits and nuts
  - Sweet and sour candy
  - Conversation hearts
  - Fresh fruit
- Let everyone make or buy their favorite cookies, such as shortbread, chocolate chip, etc. Don't forget the coffee or tea!

40

MANIFEST YOUR MIRACLE JOURNAL PROMPT

Start with something to inspire you…

- ✳ A vision board.
- ✳ A future scenario playing out or a daydream.
- ✳ You can add music and colors.
- ✳ Add a prayer—however you define it.

Next, allow yourself to find stillness and quiet. Light a candle inside or a fire outdoors.

This can last any time from ten minutes to as long as you are able.

Make sure you have paper and pen. Allow yourself to write freely without putting the pen down. While you are writing, let yourself be at ease, using your prayer to guide you through as the ink hits the page. Make any last adjustments to your prayer.

Keep this prayer at your altar, by your bed, or anywhere you designate as your sacred space in your home. Engage in the simple act of letting go, and your miracle will manifest.

ARTISTIC EXPRESSION

DREAM SPRAY

One of Ally's favorite times of the week is her yoga class with Miss Alicia. She loves her grounding yoga flow, and like most yogis, her favorite pose is savasana!

In relaxation pose, her yoga teacher always has her dream spray handy. It relaxes and calms the body while having downtime.

We wanted to share the make-at-home recipe for you to use any time for calming moments, to spray on your pillow, or just use anytime you need it.

HOW TO CREATE YOUR DREAM SPRAY:

Super simple and easy!

- Purchase small spray bottles at your local craft store
- Purchase distilled water
- Obtain essential oils (We love lavender and vanilla, but feel free to use any scent that appeals to you.)
- You may also add witch hazel to certain batches. If you would like to make it a face toner, with rose oil it is glorious.
- Add distilled water and fill the bottle, leaving room for 5 drops of each oil, shake and mist!
- For toner, use one part witch hazel, one part distilled water. Spritz on face for clarity and rejuvenation to tone skin.
- Depending on how strong you like the scent, you can adjust the oil drops.
- Be blissful!

SPRING

MAY ALL BEINGS BE FREE!

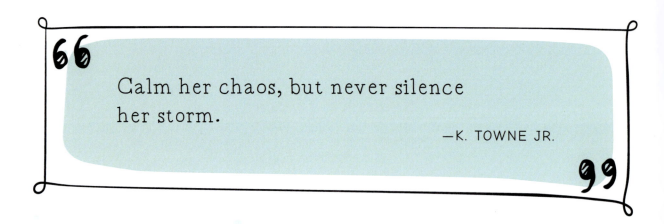

> "Calm her chaos, but never silence her storm."
>
> —K. TOWNE JR.

CEREAL GIRL

She loves a good bowl of cereal. Even on Thanksgiving Day. Cheerios are the go to, then Rice and Corn Chex...Mini Wheats.

And on a splurge she may go with Corn Pops.

I shouldn't say bowl...more like a box. A sitting and movement routine to take time and prepare.

It's what she likes to do independently— and she is so very proud.

She gets her bowl, spoon, milk from the fridge, and pours her choice until the milk almost overflows. Then happily walks away...until there is milk showing in the bowl and then she's back. Cereal now falling to the side of the bowl. She runs off again.

Content. Grounded. Eating cereal.

Simplicity.

Sometimes you just need a simple food choice where you feel settled and at home.

At night as a snack—The perfect late night dinner for Moms...the perfect dinner when there is no dinner.

It begins when you place Cheerios on the high-chair table and watch your sweet toddler scoop them up, and finally you get to sit too.

Then it's the quick go-to breakfast when they're off to grammar school—and NOW you can get your own cereal—you sweet Cheerio girl.

Back to simplicity. It's in these moments that happiness cries out in my kitchen—watching independence grow to someone who worked so hard to learn how to use a spoon.

Let's invite simplicity into our world every day. We can find this in small experiences and simple meals. It's one of Ally's core teachings. "Keep it Simple Mommy!!!"

Remember, connection comes when you slow down. Pull back from the crowds and madness and remember—

In stillness is where we receive.

Stay Radiant ✨❤️✨

SPRING 00

WATERCOLOR EXPRESSION JOURNAL PROMPT

We love the freedom of painting with watercolors. Dip your brush
in the water and create your own masterpieces.

Blending and mixing allows you to expand and settle into any mood as you paint.

Express yourself—Find inspiration from the doodles in this book
and create your own. Note which colors inspire you.

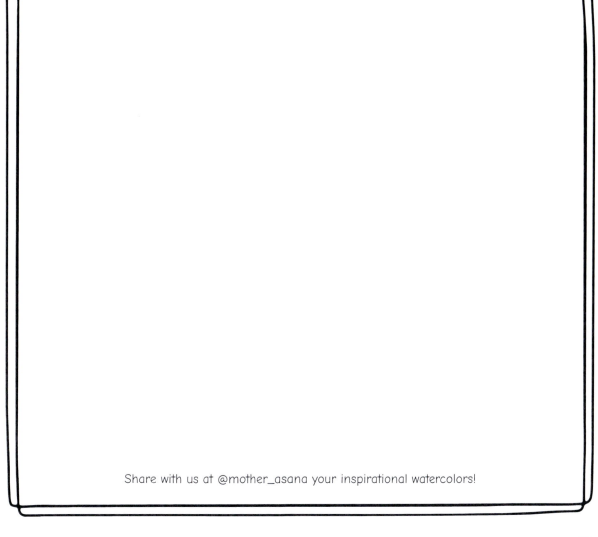

Share with us at @mother_asana your inspirational watercolors!

SPRING

ARTISTIC EXPRESSION
CEREAL RAINBOWS

WHAT YOU NEED:

- Grab your favorite brand of colored cereal!
- Some example are: Froot Loops, Fruity Pebbles, Apple Jacks, Trix, Fruity Cheerios, or Lucky Charms
- Regular glue
- Crayons or markers for the pot of gold

TO CREATE:

- Assemble your favorite cereal into the shape of a rainbow!
- Glue one, then eat one!
- Allow time for drying
- Display!

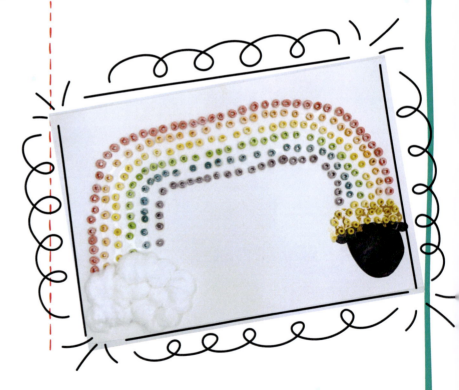

Share your cereal rainbows with us at @mother_asana

THE ART & VOICE OF AUTISM

REFERENCES

PAGE 10:

Barney — https://www.songlyrics.com/barney/mr-sun-lyrics/

PAGE 12:

ET, directed by Steven Spielberg (1982; United States: Universal Pictures and Amblin Productions, 1982), DVD.

Jaws, directed by Steven Spielberg (1975; United States: Universal Pictures, 1975), DVD.

Ferris Bueller's Day Off, directed by John Hughes (1986; United States: Paramount Pictures, 1975), DVD.

Grease, directed by Randal Kleiser (1978; United States: Paramount Pictures, 1978), DVD.

Finding Dory, directed by Andrew Stanton (2016; United States: Walt Disney Pictures and Pixar Animation Studio, 2016), DVD.

The Little Mermaid, directed by Ron Clements and John Musker (1989; Walt Disney Pictures, Walt Disney feature Animation, and Silver Screen Partners IV, 1989), DVD.

Oreo is a trademark of INTERCONTINENTAL GREAT BRANDS LLC.

Ziploc is a trademark of S. C. JOHNSON & SON, INC.

PAGE 14:

Barney Home Video: What a World We Share 1999. Added September 22, 2013. YouTube video, 53:01. https://youtu.be/35vSpZUOmHQ.

Walmart is a trademark of WAL-MART STORES, INC

Chodron, Pema. Tonglen, the Path of Transformation. Halifax NS: Vajradhatu Publications, 2001.

PAGE 16:

Trader Joe's is the trademark of Trader Joe's Company.

L.L. Bean is the trademark of L.L. Bean, Inc.

PAGE 18:

Henry James — https://www.goodreads.com/quotes/63388-summer-afternoon-summer-afternoon-to-me-those-have-always-been-the

PAGE 20:

Mod-Podge is a trademark of PLAID ENTERPRISES, INC.

PAGE 22

Graham Kendrick, "Shine Jesus Shine." Recorded May 4, 2019. YouTube video, 4:30. https://www.youtube.com/watch?v=7_HShjOtHBQ.

PAGE 30:

Barney — https://www.songlyrics.com/barney/my-family-s-just-right-for-me-lyrics/

49

MOTHER ASANA

PAGE 34:

Alice in Wonderland — https://www.goodreads.com/quotes/815118-i-knew-who-i-was-this-morning-but-i-ve-changed

PAGE 36

Saran wrap is a trademark of Mobi, Inc.

PAGE 38:

E.E. Cummings — https://www.goodreads.com/quotes/17533-i-carry-your-heart-with-me-i-carry-it-in

Netflix is a trademark of Netflix, Inc.

Course in Miracles

All quotes are from A Course in Miracles, copyright ©1992, 1999, 2007 by the Foundation for Inner Peace, 448 Ignacio Blvd., #306, Novato, CA 94949, www.acim.org and info@acim.org, used with permission.

PAGE 42:

Rumi — https://www.goodreads.com/quotes/60617-you-wander-from-room-to-room-hunting-for-the-diamond

Kleenex is a trademark of Kimberly-Clark Worldwide, Inc.

iPad is a trademark of APPLE INC.

PAGE 44:

The recipe for dream spray is used with permission from Alicia Berger Harriman, "Miss Alicia" from Stretch Therapy in Connectivut, http://stretchtherapyct.com/team.

PAGE 46:

K Towne Jr. — https://www.yourtango.com/2016290788/22-love-quotes-instagrams-most-romantic-poet

Cheerios is a trademark of GENERAL MILLS IP HOLDINGS I, LLC.

Rice Chex is a trademark of GARDETTO'S BAKERY, INC.

Corn Chex is a trademark of GARDETTO'S BAKERY, INC.

Mini Wheats is a trademark of KELLOGG NORTH AMERICA COMPANY.

Corn Pops is a trademark of KELLOGG NORTH AMERICA COMPANY.

PAGE 48:

Froot Loops is a trademark of KELLOGG NORTH AMERICA COMPANY.

Fruity Pebbles is a trademark of Hanna-Barbera Productions, Inc.

Apple Jacks is a trademark of KELLOGG NORTH AMERICA COMPANY.

Trix is a trademark of GENERAL MILLS IP HOLDINGS II, LLC.

Fruity Cheerios is a trademark of GENERAL MILLS IP HOLDINGS I, LLC.

Lucky Charms is a trademark of GENERAL MILLS IP HOLDINGS I, LLC.